Published by Periplus Editions with editorial offices at
130 Joo Seng Road #06-01, Singapore 368357 and
153 Milk Street, Boston, Massachusetts 02109.

LCC Card No: 2004110731
ISBN 0-7946-0339-4
Text © 2005 Periplus Editions (HK) Ltd
Illustrations © 2005 Marijke den Ouden
Art Direction and Design by Marijke den Ouden

Printed in Singapore

Distributed by:

North America, Latin America & Europe:
Tuttle Publishing, 364 Innovation Drive,
North Clarendon, VT 05759-9436, USA
Tel: (802) 773 8930; fax: (802) 773 6993
Email: info@tuttlepublishing.com
Website: www.tuttlepublishing.com

Asia Pacific: Berkeley Books Pte Ltd,
130 Joo Seng Road #06-01, Singapore 368357
Tel: (65) 6280 1330; fax: (65) 6280 6290
Email: inquiries@periplus.com.sg
Website: www.periplus.com

Indonesia: PT Java Books Indonesia,
Jl. Kelapa Gading Kirana, Blok A-14/17, Jakarta 14240
Tel: (021) 451 5351; fax: (021) 453 4987
Email: cs@javabooks.co.id

Japan: Tuttle Publishing,
Yaekari Building 3F, 5-4-12 Osaki,
Shinagawa-ku, Tokyo 141-0032
Tel: (03) 5437 0171; fax: (03) 5437 0755
Email: tuttle-sales@gol.com

13 12 11 10 09 08 07 06 05
9 8 7 6 5 4 3 2 1

Fun with Asian Food

A Kids' Cookbook

Recipes **Devagi Sanmugam** • Illustrations **Marijke den Ouden**

PERIPLUS EDITIONS

Singapore • Hong Kong • Indonesia

Cooking Asian Food

is easy and fun!

Contents

Welcome to the exciting world of Asian cooking and culture! The recipes in this book allow you to create a whole range of interesting new tastes from every corner of exotic Asia. Yet these dishes are all incredibly easy to make, and they require for the most part common ingredients that are available now in most well-stocked supermarkets. Recipes with one or two stars in the row of icons are the easiest to prepare. The clear, step-by-step instructions and illustrations will guide you. At all times follow the preparation and safety tips, and have fun!

Good preparation is important

Obtain an adult's permission to use the kitchen. It's a good idea to have an older brother or sister or a parent to help as well. Before you start cooking, get out all of the ingredients and utensils you will need. Each recipe contains drawings of the utensils needed.

Read the whole recipe several times and make sure you really understand it. Follow the recipe exactly.

Always work clean

Before starting, wash your hands with soap and water. Wash your hands again after you handle raw meat, eggs or fish. Always wash your hands before you eat and after you go to the bathroom.

Be sure to use a clean knife, spoon or fork. Don't just pick one up from the counter or kitchen sink.

Don't sneeze or cough on food. Keep hands away from your face and hair and pets. If you touch your pet, wash your hands before touching food again.

Wear clean clothes or a clean apron. Keep the cooking area clean as you cook. If you spill something, quickly wipe it up.

When touching foods with your hands, do not to lick your fingers or put a finger in your mouth. This is especially important when touching raw foods, such as dough and meat, because when still uncooked they may contain harmful bacteria.

Be sure to work safely

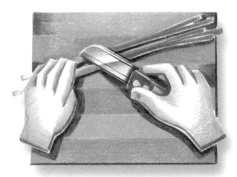

Watch out for sharp knives. Let an adult cut or slice foods or help you do it.

Use oven mitts or pot holders when taking food out of the oven or cooking on the stove.

Turn pan handles toward the back of the stove so you don't knock into it by accident.

Don't wear clothes with big, loose sleeves when you cook. They can cause accidents.

Keep electrical appliances away from water to avoid shocks.

Stay away from electrical sockets, especially if your hands are wet.

Turn off the oven and all cooking appliances as soon as you finish cooking. Double check again before you leave the kitchen.

Keep paper towels, dish towels and pot holders away from the stove so they don't catch on fire.

Handle food with care

Keep products like milk, butter, meat, poultry and eggs cold. Don't leave them out of the refrigerator while you are cooking or eating. Perishable foods should not be kept at room temperature for more than two hours.

Always use a clean plate. Never put cooked food on an unwashed plate or a cutting board that has had raw food on it.

Emergencies

If you have a small fire in the kitchen, have an adult put a lid on the pot or pour baking soda on the fire. Be sure you know where the baking soda is before you start cooking. If the fire is in the oven, do not open the door until the fire completely stops.

If you burn yourself, tell an adult immediately and hold the burned area under cool running water.

How do you know if you like what you eat?

Your tongue and the roof of your mouth are covered with thousands of tiny tastebuds. These tastebuds help your brain tell you what you are tasting. The saliva in your mouth helps break down your food, and then messages are sent through sensory nerves to your brain.

The stars in the boxes tell you how difficult the recipe is. One star is the easiest.

The icons are safety reminders and give the approximate preparation and cooking times.

Ask an adult to be present.

Wash your hands before you start.

Be careful when using a knife.

Be careful when using the stove.

Be careful when using electricity.

Be careful when using the oven.

Preparation and cooking time.

15 min

Indian Fruit Lassi

The Fruit Lassi is one of India's favorite drinks—made with yogurt and fresh fruit. In summer, ice is added. A *lassi* is an Indian version of a milkshake and depending on the ingredients used it can be a Mango Lassi, a Strawberry Lassi or a Banana Lassi. The recipe given here adds silken tofu for extra protein.

Ingredients

1½ cups (8 oz/250 g) fresh or frozen strawberries
½ packet silken tofu (4 oz/125 g)
1½ cups (375 ml) plain yogurt
15 ice cubes
3 tablespoons honey or sugar
2 tablespoons shelled unsalted pistachio nuts
4 extra strawberries and 4 sprigs of mint leaves, to garnish (optional)

Utensils

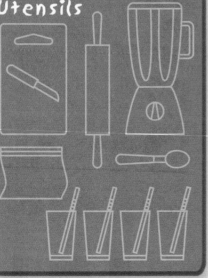

Anneke and Max are twins who enjoy cooking Asian food and love dressing up in *costumes* from the Asian countries where all this tasty food comes from.

Anneke is wearing a colorful Indian *dance* costume. Around her ankles and waist she wears bells that make a rhythmic sound when she dances. Indian dance has been around for over 2,000 years and the dances are based on themes from India's rich culture.

10 min

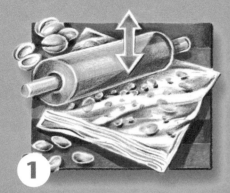

1 Put the shelled pistachio nuts in a small plastic bag and break the nuts into small pieces using a rolling pin. Put to one side.

2 Wash the strawberries and remove their leaves and crowns. Set 4 strawberries aside and slice the rest. Divide the washed mint into 4 small sprigs.

How about a
Papaya
Lassi?

10 oz (300 g) ripe papaya
2 tablespoons rolled oats
1/2 packet silken tofu (4 oz/125 g)
1 1/2 cups (375 ml) plain yogurt
3 tablespoons honey or sugar
15 ice cubes

3 Place the sliced strawberries, tofu, yogurt, ice cubes and honey or sugar in a blender. Blend until smooth, about 5 minutes.

4 Pour the mixture into glasses and sprinkle each one with the crushed pistachios. Decorate each glass with 1 slit strawberry and a mint sprig. Serve with a straw.

Cut the papaya in half. Scoop out the seeds and discard. Scoop out the papaya flesh and cut into cubes. Process all ingredients in a blender for 5 minutes.

Some more great flavors to try!

Mango
Lassi

Flesh of 1 ripe mango
2 tablespoons blanched almonds
1/4 teaspoon ground cardamom
    or cinnamon (optional)
1/2 packet silken tofu (4 oz/125 g)
1 1/2 cups (375 ml) plain yogurt
3 tablespoons honey or sugar
15 ice cubes

See the Filipino mango pudding recipe at page 27 for guidance as to how to cut the mango. Process all ingredients in a blender for 5 minutes.

Banana
Lassi

2 ripe bananas
2 tablespoons shelled unsalted
    pistachio nuts
1/2 packet silken tofu (4 oz/125 g)
1 1/2 cups (375 ml) plain yogurt
3 tablespoons honey or sugar
15 ice cubes

Peel the bananas and shell the pistachios. Crush the shelled pistachios. Process all ingredients in a blender for 5 minutes.

Japanese Egg Custard Cups

In Japan these egg cups are called **Chawan Mushi**, which means "teacup custard," because the custard is steamed in small teacups. The tasty custard usually contains *dashi*, a soup stock made from dried bonito flakes and kelp seaweed.

Chawan Mushi is soft, like pudding, and you can add some vegetables or even shrimp. Serve each person with their own cup and a small spoon.

Chawan Mushi teacups have beautiful decorations and a lid to keep the food warm.

Anneke is wearing a Japanese kimono just like a *geisha*. Geishas are women who provide musical and dancing entertainment. Anneke has pretty flowers in her hair and she is fanning herself. Look at that white makeup on her face!

Ingredients

2 shiitake mushrooms (fresh or dried) or 4 button mushrooms
3 medium eggs
1 cup (250 ml) chicken stock or dashi stock
1/2 teaspoon salt
1/2 teaspoon soy sauce
4 fresh shrimp, peeled
Rind of 1/2 lemon to garnish (optional)

Utensils

35 min

4 Pieces

Try it!

These egg cups are a fun way to prepare your eggs! The cups can also be steamed in a microwave (medium to high heat)—but use paper towels to cover them instead of foil.

1 Wipe the mushrooms clean with a paper towel. (If using dried mushrooms, soak them in warm water first for 10 minutes.) Discard the stems and thinly slice the caps.

2 Preheat the oven to 350°F (180°C). Using a fine grater, grate the outer layer of skin from the lemon. Place the grated lemon rind in a saucer.

3 Carefully crack the eggs into a mixing bowl. Crack the middle of the eggs on the rim of the bowl and make sure no shells get into the bowl.

4 Very gently beat the eggs and draw the letter Z on the bottom with the tip of the chopsticks, to avoid air bubbles or foam from forming.

5 Mix the chicken stock or dashi stock, salt and soy sauce together in a measuring cup.

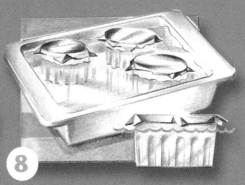

6 Little by little add the chicken stock or dashi stock mixture to the beaten eggs.

7 Use 4 small oven-proof cups or teacups. Divide the mushrooms and shrimp equally into the 4 cups. Pour in the egg mixture. Sprinkle each cup with a little grated lemon rind. Cover the cups with aluminium foil.

8 Place the cups into a baking pan. Pour water into the pan until it comes up to $\frac{3}{4}$ of the height of the cups. Place the dish in a preheated oven and bake at 350°F (180°C) for 20 minutes. Remove carefully and serve.

Tropical Thai Chicken Soup

Ingredients

1 chicken breast, skin removed
$\frac{1}{2}$ lemon
2 tablespoons lime juice
2 tablespoons soy sauce
7 oz (200 g) cauliflower
10 fresh basil leaves
3 to 4 baby carrots, sliced
2 slices fresh ginger root
2 stalks lemongrass
3 cups (750 ml) chicken stock
1 teaspoon curry powder
1 cup (250 ml) coconut
  milk or skimmed milk
$\frac{1}{4}$ teaspoon salt
1 teaspoon sugar
Finely sliced fresh chili or
  chili flakes (optional)
2 sprigs coriander
  leaves (cilantro)

Utensils

Tropical Thai Chicken Soup was Max's favorite dish on his last trip to Thailand. Thai food is very different from Indian or Chinese food, and uses a lot of coconut milk, spices and lemongrass.

Max had a great time in Thailand—it's a beautiful country with clean beaches, and the sun shines all year round. The people are very friendly and there are lots of awesome Buddhist temples.

Coconut milk gives a rich creamy taste to dishes. It's an important ingredient for Thai curries, soups and sweets. Coconut milk is available in cans or cartons, or can be made fresh from the grated flesh of a coconut by adding water and squeezing it.

⭐⭐ 👁 ✍ 🔪 🔥 ◔

45 min

Lemon-grass

Lemongrass gives a mild lemony flavor to dishes. Usually it's not eaten and should be removed once the soup has been cooked.

1 Place the chicken breast on a cutting board and cut the chicken into small, bite-sized pieces. Wash the cutting board.

2 Grate the outer skin of the lemon using a fine grater. Squeeze the lime juice. Slice the coriander leaves (cilantro) and set everything aside.

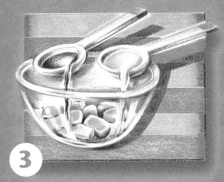

3 Place the chicken pieces into a mixing bowl and pour in the soy sauce and lime juice. Mix with a spoon. Cover and set aside for 10 minutes to marinate.

4 Cut the cauliflower into small florets. Remove the stems from the basil leaves. Wash the carrots and slice. Keep aside on a plate.

5 Peel one end of the ginger root. Cut off two thin slices. Using a knife, cut off the top two thirds of the lemongrass leaving only the thick bottom third and slice this part into small round pieces.

6 Place the chicken stock, chicken pieces, vegetables, curry powder, lemongrass and ginger slices in a saucepan. Bring to a boil, reduce the heat to low, and simmer for 10 minutes until the chicken changes color.

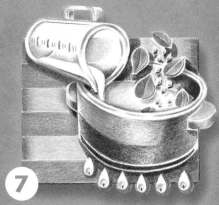

7 Pour the coconut milk or skimmed milk into the pan and add the basil leaves, the grated lemon rind, salt and sugar. Simmer for 5 minutes and stir with a wooden spoon while it is simmering.

8 Turn off the heat and remove the pan from the stove. With a spoon or tongs, remove the lemongrass pieces—these are not to be eaten. Serve in bowls sprinkled with chili flakes or chili (if using) and coriander leaves (cilantro).

Korean
Vegetable Pancakes

Korean pancakes are delicious and nutritious snacks that can be eaten any time of the day, or as appetizers with meals.

Ingredients

1 cup (5 oz/150 g) plain flour
Dash of ground white pepper
1 teaspoon salt
$\frac{1}{2}$ teaspoon sesame oil
1 cup (250 ml) water
3 spring onions
4 teaspoons cooking oil for frying
1 cup (1$\frac{1}{2}$ oz/50 g) beansprouts
$\frac{1}{2}$ carrot, grated

Dipping Sauce

3 tablespoons soy sauce
1$\frac{1}{2}$ tablespoons vinegar
1$\frac{1}{2}$ tablespoons sugar
1 teaspoon sesame oil
1 teaspoon toasted sesame seeds (optional)

Utensils

4x

Anneke is wearing a colorful *hanbok*. It has a long skirt and a blouse-like top with long sleeves. At family celebrations or special occasions, Korean girls like to dress up in their fanciest *hanbok*

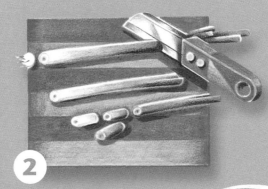

4 Pieces

Dipping Sauce

1

Combine the flour, pepper, salt and sesame oil in a mixing bowl. Make a well in the center and pour the water into it. Using a wooden spoon, stir until it forms a thick, lump-free batter.

2

Wash the spring onions, then place them on a cutting board and cut them into ½ inch (1 cm) lengths. Throw away the roots and tops.

Make the dipping sauce by combining all the ingredients in a serving bowl and put it on the table.

3

Place a small skillet on the stove and add 1 teaspoon of cooking oil. Turn the heat to medium. Wait about a minute until the pan and oil heat up.

4

Using a cup or ladle, scoop about ⅓ of a cup (85 ml) of the batter and pour it into the skillet. Using the back of the ladle or a large spoon, spread the batter into a round pancake.

5

Sprinkle some of the cut spring onions onto the pancake. Fry on one side until golden brown (about 3 or 4 minutes), but take care not to let the pancake burn.

6

Use a spatula to turn the pancake over when one side is cooked. If the skillet gets too hot, reduce the heat a little.

7

Sprinke some of the beansprouts and grated carrot on the pancake. Let the pancake cook for about 1 minute on this side.

8

Fold the pancake in half and lift it out onto a serving plate. Repeat for the other pancakes. Serve with the dipping sauce.

You can also try adding other fillings in your pancakes

Japanese Bread Sushi

Have you ever heard of sushi? Most cities around the world now have *sushi bars* that serve lots of different kinds of sushi. Sushi is from Japan, and is normally made with seasoned rice that is rolled up with fish and seaweed, but our recipe uses bread instead. Use only a small amount of *wasabi*—it has a strong taste.

Max is wearing a Japanese summer cotton kimono called a *yukata*. "Kimono" means clothing in Japanese and a yukata is a simple one that is worn at home. Nowadays the yukata is considered casual leisure wear and is very comfortable, worn by both men and women. Wooden sandals are often worn with a yukata—look at Max's!

Expert Japanese **sushi chefs** need many years of training, but with this easy recipe you can become an expert right away!

Nori is a kind of dried *seaweed* that is sold in sheets or flakes.

Ingredients

½ cucumber
2 bread slices (white or whole wheat bread)
2 chicken hotdogs or 2 tablespoons canned tuna flakes
2 toasted nori seaweed sheets
2 teaspoons cream cheese
¼ teaspoon wasabi or mustard

Utensils

8 Pieces

Pink, Red, Yellow!

Sushi can be made with lots of colorful ingredients; pink shrimp or tuna, white fish and yellow eggs.

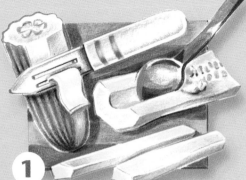

1

Peel the cucumber and cut it in half lengthwise. Using a spoon, scrape out the seeds. Cut the cucumber into long, thin strips—about $1/2$ inch (1 cm) thick and 4 inches (10 cm) long.

2

Place the bread slices on a cutting board and trim off the crusts. Slightly press the bread slices with your clean hand to flatten them.

3

Place the hotdogs in a saucepan with water. Prick them with a fork. Turn on the stove and cook for 2 minutes. (Or use canned ready-to-eat hotdogs.)

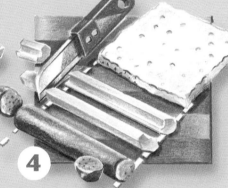

4

Trim both the hotdogs and the cucumber sticks to the width of the bread. Cut the hotdogs into strips if they are too thick.

5

Place a sheet of nori on the cutting board. Place one of the bread slices on it. Using a pair of scissors, trim the nori sheet, leaving one end of the nori a bit longer than the bread.

6

Mix the cream cheese and wasabi or mustard in a small bowl. Then with a bread knife, spread half of it on one side of the slice of bread.

7

Arrange a strip of cucumber and a hotdog (or 1 tablespoon of tuna flakes) along one edge of the bread. Roll the nori around the bread tightly so the longer edge wraps up all the way around it.

8

Using your finger, put a tiny bit of water on the inside of the nori so it sticks. Cut the roll into 4 pieces and place them on a plate. Repeat with the other bread and ingredients to make a total of 8 sushi pieces.

Cantonese Wonton Soup

The Chinese like to wrap bits of vegetables and meat in *dumplings* called wontons, and boil them in soup.

Max is a *Chinese opera* singer, playing the part of a general and wearing heavy makeup.

Ingredients

3 mushrooms
10 to 15 spinach leaves
8 bok choy or lettuce leaves
$^1/_2$ carrot, grated
1 egg white
5 to 6 tablespoons of ricotta or cottage cheese (4 oz/125 g)
$^1/_4$ teaspoon salt
$1^1/_2$ teaspoons sesame oil
$^1/_2$ teaspoon sugar
2 teaspoons cornstarch
7 oz (200 g) ground chicken or pork
16 wonton wrappers
6 cups ($1^1/_2$ liters) chicken stock or 1 tablespoon soup stock granules dissolved in 6 cups of water ($1^1/_2$ liters)
1 tablespoon soy sauce

Utensils

40 min

4 Bowls

Bok Choy

Bok Choy is a leafy green vegetable. You can use choy sum or lettuce leaves instead.

1

Wipe the mushrooms clean with a paper towel. Discard the stems and thinly slice the caps on a cutting board. Wash the spinach and remove the stems. Thinly slice the spinach leaves.

2

Separate and wash the bok choy leaves or lettuce leaves, pat dry and cut them into pieces. Peel the washed carrot and grate it coarsely.

3

Carefully crack the eggshell (over the bowl's rim). Put the egg into one of your hands. Let the egg white drop through your fingers into the bowl. Discard the egg yolk.

4

Wash your hands again. Add the diced mushrooms, sliced spinach, grated carrot, cheese, salt, 1/2 teaspoon of the sesame oil, sugar, cornstarch and ground meat to the bowl with the egg white.

5

Place a wonton wrapper on a plate or cutting board. Scoop 2 teaspoons of the filling onto the center of the wrapper. Fold the edges together and lightly pinch the edges so they stick together.

6

Heat the chicken stock in a saucepan and add the soy sauce and the remaining 1 teaspoon of the sesame oil. Once it starts to boil, turn the heat down to low.

7

Using a spoon, gently place the wontons into the simmering soup. Once the wontons float to the surface, add the bok choy or lettuce. Do not overcook the bok choy.

8

When the bok choy leaves turn bright green, turn off the heat. Using a cup or ladle, carefully transfer the soup and the wontons to soup bowls and serve.

Vietnamese Spring Rolls

The beauty of Vietnamese Spring Rolls is that they have lots of herbs and vegetables and plenty of flavor—but don't have to be fried! You can use shrimp or pork or chicken sausage or fried tofu as the main ingredient, and snow peas can be added instead of carrots.

Rice paper wrappers are made from rice flour, and they are dried in the sun on bamboo baskets. Before using, soak in water to soften (but no need to cook them).

Ingredients

- $1/2$ lemon
- $1^1/_2$ tablespoons chunky peanut butter
- 1 teaspoon superfine caster sugar or honey
- 8 cooked and peeled shrimp, or prawns, or $1/2$ cooked chicken breast
- 4 spring onions
- 6 cabbage or lettuce leaves
- 1 cup ($1^1/_2$ oz/50 g) beansprouts
- 1 small carrot, grated
- 8 dried rice paper wrappers or 8 large lettuce leaves
- 8 basil leaves
- 8 mint leaves

Utensils

This recipe is best made fresh just before eating since the rice paper dries out if you let it sit for too long.

25 min

4 Pieces

Any Time

These spring rolls are very easy to make and perfect for a light meal or as an appetizer.

1 Squeeze the lemon and measure 2 teaspoons of juice into a mixing bowl. Add the peanut butter and sugar or honey. Stir with a spoon to mix well.

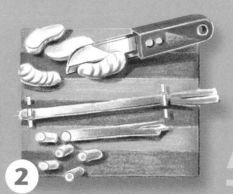

2 Cut the shrimp in half lengthwise and cut the spring onions into small pieces. If using cooked chicken instead of shrimp, cut it into 16 thin strips.

3 Wash the cabbage or lettuce leaves and shake them dry. Stack the leaves and roll them up. Slice them into thin strips.

4 Wash the beansprouts and shake them dry. Peel the washed carrot and grate it coarsely.

5 Place the rice paper wrappers in a dish. Pour in enough water to cover them and soak for 1 to 2 minutes. Drain out the water.

Try spring rolls wrapped in lettuce leaves—nice and crunchy!

6 Carefully peel off 2 of the soaked wrappers and put them on top of each other (on a clean cutting board or plate). Spread ½ tablespoon of the peanut butter mixture in a straight line on the top wrapper.

7 Place 4 pieces of the shrimp or chicken, a few pieces of all the vegetables, 2 basil leaves and 2 mint leaves over the sauce to form a rectangular mound.

8 Fold one side of the wrapper over the filling, then fold in both the ends, then roll it up tightly and seal using a tiny bit of water. Place on a serving plate. Repeat steps 6 to 8 to make the other 3 rolls.

Delicious Naan Pizza

Wow, yummy pizza made with freshly baked *Indian* naan bread or Middle Eastern pita bread. Mmmm ... nothing could be more delicious.

Ingredients
2 small ripe tomatoes
4 button mushrooms
4 rings canned pineapple
1 cup (4 oz/125 g) cooked ham or chicken or turkey or sausage
4 naan breads or pita breads
4 tablespoons sweet mango chutney or tomato ketchup
1 tablespoon dried basil or oregano leaves
1 cup (7 oz/200 g) grated cheddar or mozzarella cheese
1 tablespoon minced coriander leaves (cilantro), to garnish (optional)

Utensils

4x

Naan is an Indian flat bread that is oval in shape and cooked in a *tandoor* or clay oven. They can be bought freshly made from Indian restaurants or frozen or vacuum packed from supermarkets.

Can you recognize Max? He's dressed as a traditional Indian farmer today! On Max's head is a bright red *turban* and he has a wavy false moustache. The turban is made from a very long piece of cloth that is wrapped around Max's head. Max is eating a piece of naan bread. Indians eat this flat bread with their meals. Naan is one of the most popular Indian breads. A trip to an Indian restaurant usually involves ordering some kind of naan.

4 Pizzas

1

Preheat the oven to 400°F (200°C). Wash the tomatoes and slice them thinly. Wipe the mushrooms clean with a paper towel, cut off and discard the stems and thinly slice the caps.

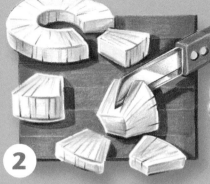

2

Drain the pineapple rings and press them between paper towels to squeeze out the juice. Cut them into small chunks.

Try it!

Your friends will be really impressed if you serve them these homemade pizzas!

3

Cut the meat into small pieces.

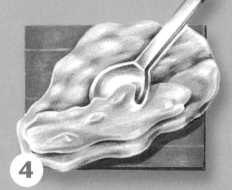

4

Place the naan or pita breads on a baking sheet. Spread equal amounts of mango chutney or tomato ketchup on the naan breads. Sprinkle with the basil or oregano leaves.

5

Arrange the tomato slices on the breads, then the pineapple chuncks, meat and mushroom slices.

6

Use grated cheese or make your own by grating the cheese with a coarse grater.

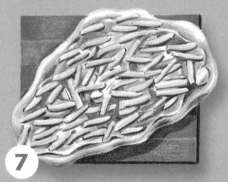

7

Sprinkle the pizza with cheese and bake in a preheated oven at 400°F (200°C) for 15 minutes or until the cheese has melted completely.

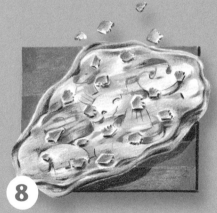

8

Using an oven mitt, remove the pizzas from the oven. Lightly sprinkle with the minced coriander leaves (cilantro) if using. Serve warm on a plate.

Longevity Birthday Noodles

Noodles are thought to have been invented in China, where they are a popular dish to celebrate birthdays. The *long strands* of noodles represent long life.

Ingredients

- 10 oz (300 g) dry egg noodles, ramen or fine spaghetti
- 5 oz (150 g) fresh or frozen spinach leaves
- 2 cups (4 oz/125 g) sliced snow peas
- $1/2$ cup (100 g/about 4 heaping tablespoons) peanut butter or tahini paste
- $1/4$ cup (60 ml) hot water (use more if needed)
- 4 tablespoons soy sauce
- Juice of 1 lemon or lime
- 3 tablespoons fine sugar
- 3 spring onions or chives

Utensils

Eating noodles with chopsticks can be challenging! But with a bit of practice you can become a real pro at it. Made from wheat or rice or even beans, *Noodles* can be eaten hot or cold, boiled, steamed, stir-fried, deep-fried, or in a soup. Noodles are served at Chinese New Year.

Max is wearing a traditional Chinese New Year outfit. The *dragon* image represents strength, happiness and immortality, and the red and gold colors are said to bring good fortune.

20 min

4 Bowls

1

Prepare the noodles or spaghetti according to the directions on the package. Ask an adult to help you to drain the noodles in the sink using a colander.

2

Remove the spinach stems and wash the leaves well to remove any sand or dirt. Wash and slice the snow peas. Place the spinach and snow peas in a small saucepan and add 2 cups of water. Blanch them for 1 minute until they turn bright green.

Tahini

If using tahini paste, increase the sugar to 5 tablespoons.

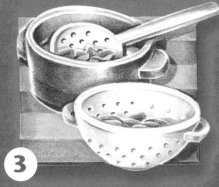

3

Drain the vegetables in the sink either using a colander or a large strainer. Set to one side. Squeeze the lemon.

Long Noodles, Long Life

Instead of eating cake, the Chinese enjoy a big helping of "long life" noodles on their birthday — the longer the noodles, the longer your life!

4

In a mixing bowl, combine the peanut butter or tahini paste with the hot water, soy sauce, lemon juice and sugar. Mix well, using a spoon or a whisk.

5

Place the noodles in the same mixing bowl as the sauce. Mix well, using a fork or a pair of chopsticks.

6

Place the spring onions or chives on a cutting board and cut off and discard the roots and tops. Cut the rest into small pieces.

7

Serve the noodles in 4 serving bowls. Garnish with the blanched spinach, snow peas and spring onions. Serve immediately.

Singapore
Chicken Rice Meatballs

These rice balls, the size of table tennis or golf balls, are an enjoyable variation on a popular Singapore dish called chicken rice. Originally brought to Singapore by Chinese *immigrants*— this dish is a delicious combination of chicken and rice and served with a specially made chili sauce. Instead of chicken, try using drained canned tuna.

Max is wearing traditional clogs and a Chinese shirt with Chinese *buttons*

Ingredients

- 1½ cups (10 oz/300 g) uncooked rice
- 1½ teaspoons salt
- 2 cups (500 ml) boiling water
- 3 cloves garlic, minced
- 2 spring onions
- 1 small carrot, grated
- 10 oz (300 g) ground chicken
- 1 tablespoon soy sauce
- 1 teaspoon sesame oil
- 3 teaspoons cornstarch
- ½ teaspoon sugar
- 5 or 6 lettuce or cabbage leaves (optional)

Utensils

1 hour   30 min

16 Pieces

Steamed Dishes

Bamboo baskets are used in Singapore to steam dishes, but any steamer can be used.

1

In a bowl, wash the rice with water until the water runs clear. Then cover the rice with water and let it soak for about 1 hour. Drain the rice with a sieve.

2

Place the rice into a bowl. Add 1 teaspoon of salt and carefully pour boiling water over the rice. Set aside to cool. Strain in a sieve.

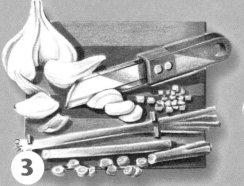

3

Using a cutting board, peel the garlic cloves and finely mince with a knife. Wash and cut the spring onions into small pieces. Put the garlic and spring onions in a large mixing bowl.

4

Wash, peel and grate the carrot. Put the grated carrot in the same mixing bowl as the garlic and spring onions.

5

Place the ground chicken, soy sauce, sesame oil, cornstarch, sugar and the remaining $1/2$ teaspoon of salt into the mixing bowl. Using a large spoon, mix well to combine all the ingredients.

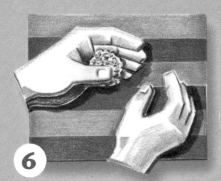

6

Wet your hands. Scoop a tablespoon of the mixture and form it into a ball about 1 inch (2.5 cm) in diameter and place the ball on a plate. Repeat with the rest of the mixture.

7

Grease a steamer tray with oil or line with lettuce or cabbage leaves. On a plate, roll the chicken balls in the drained rice and make sure they are thoroughly coated. Arrange them on the steamer tray, leaving some space between each ball.

8

Place the steamer tray in a steamer filled half-way with water. Close the steamer with the lid and steam for 10 minutes or until the rice grains are soft and fluffy and double in size.

Grilled Chicken Yakitori Skewers

Yakitori are bite-sized pieces of chicken that have been marinated in a sweet, soy-based sauce called *teriyaki sauce*, and grilled on a skewer. Our chicken yakitori is a tasty version with chunks of chicken, apples, bell peppers and teriyaki sauce.

Ingredients
¹/₂ cup bottled teriyaki sauce
1 tablespoon sugar
1 chicken breast, skin removed
(approximately 9 oz/270 g)
1 tart green apple
1 bell pepper
8 bamboo skewers

Utensils

Max is wearing the outfit of a Japanese *samurai warrior*. The samurai followed a strict code of conduct on how to live and how to use their sword.

★★ 👁 ✋ 🔪 🍳 🕐
50 min

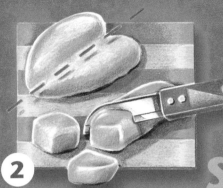

1

Preheat the oven by turning on the broiler. Pour the teriyaki sauce into a bowl. Add the sugar. Stir until the sugar dissolves.

2

Place the chicken breast on a cutting board and cut the chicken into bite-sized pieces. Wash the cutting board.

Safety Tip

Use treated skewers, or soak untreated skewers in a bowl of water for 20 minutes before using to prevent the skewers from burning.

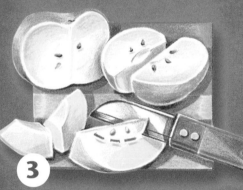

3

Cut the apple into 4 quarters. Cut out the seeds and cut each quarter into half.

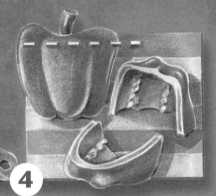

4

Cut the top off the bell pepper and cut it into four pieces.

5

Remove the seeds and cut each piece into 3 smaller pieces.

In Japan, hot charcoals are often used to grill the yakitori

6

Place the chicken, apple and bell pepper pieces into the bowl with the sauce. Stir to combine well. Allow the food to marinate for at least 15 minutes or more.

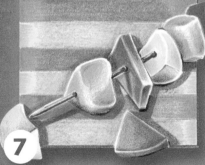

7

Thread a piece of bell pepper, a piece of chicken and a piece of apple onto a wooden skewer. Repeat one more time and then thread one piece of bell pepper. Do the same for all the skewers. Wash and dry your hands.

8

Grill the chicken skewers under the preheated broiler for 5 minutes on each side or until cooked. Be careful they don't burn, turning them more frequently if necessary. Use oven mitts when taking the tray out of the oven.

Filipino Mango Pudding

Mango Pudding made with fresh mangoes, cream and gelatin is a tasty dessert from the Philippines. *Filipino mangoes* are very sweet and juicy — and are often referred to as the king or queen of fruits.

Ingredients

2 ripe medium mangoes, (1 1/2 lbs/700 g)
1/2 cup (125 ml) mango or orange juice
3/4 cup (5 oz/150 g) sugar
2 1/2 tablespoons gelatin powder
3/4 cup (200 ml) boiling water
2/3 cup (150 ml) evaporated milk or cream
8 ice cubes

Utensils

4x

Mangoes are as common in tropical Asia as apples are in Western countries. Mangoes can be used in many different ways to make refreshing drinks and desserts, or just eaten on their own.

Anneke is wearing a lovely traditional filipino costume — a matching blouse and skirt joined at the waist. Look at those big sleeves!

1

Carefully pierce the skin of each mango on one side. Then use a spoon to peel the skin off. Peel both mangoes in this way.

2

Scoop the flesh off in small pieces. Throw away the pit (seed). Cut the flesh of one mango into dice and keep it to one side.

Ripe Mango

Some mangoes turn yellow as they ripen, but others are ripe when they are green or slightly yellow.

3

Put the flesh of the other mango in a blender and add the mango or orange juice. Process until smooth, for 2 to 3 minutes.

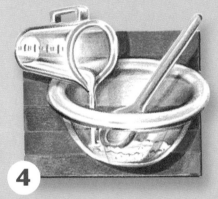

4

Combine the sugar and gelatin powder in a bowl. Mix well with a wooden spoon. Add the boiling water and stir to dissolve the gelatin and sugar.

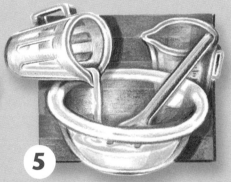

5

Add the evaporated milk or cream and the blended mango and juice. Stir well until combined.

6

Add the ice cubes and keep stirring until the ice cubes melt.

7

Using a ladle, pour the mixture into 4 small dessert bowls. Refrigerate for 2 hours until the gelatin sets.

8

To serve, carefully turn the contents of each bowl onto a plate by putting the plate face down on top of the bowl then turning them both over. Garnish with the diced mango.

15 min + 2 hours

Malaysian Pineapple Tarts

A tart is a small pie made with a delicious fruit filling. Our recipe uses pineapple jam and sweetened cream cheese, and requires no baking. Max loves these great pineapple tarts he found in Malaysia. Malaysia has lots of pineapple plantations that produce very *sweet and juicy* pineapples, and they are in plentiful supply all year round.

Max is wearing a traditional **Malay** outfit that is often worn on festive days and special occasions such as weddings. The loose-fitting shirt has a small neckline and colorful braiding will often be sewn on the collar and sleeves.

Ingredients

2 cups (9 oz/270 g) crushed graham crackers or cream crackers
3 tablespoons melted butter
1 tablespoon superfine caster sugar
Oil to grease the pan
Wax paper
4 tablespoons pineapple jam or other jam
Sweetened cream cheese

Utensils

6x

28

6 Pieces

Sweet Cream Cheese

To make sweetened cream cheese, add 2 tablespoons superfine caster sugar to 4 oz (125 g) of softened cream cheese.

1

Place the crackers into a clean plastic bag. Using a rolling pin, crush the crackers into small bits.

2

Place the crushed crackers in a mixing bowl. Add the melted butter and sugar. Stir with a wooden spoon.

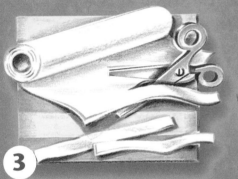

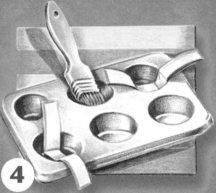

3

Cut 6 strips of wax paper that are each about 1 inch (2.5 cm) wide and 6 inches (15 cm) long.

4

Grease a muffin pan (patty tin) with oil or butter using a brush. Line each muffin mold with a strip of wax paper which sticks out on both sides.

5

Scoop enough of the crumb mixture to fill up each mold ³/₄ of the way.

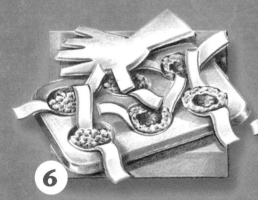

6

Using your thumb, press the crumbs to fit around the insides of the mold, creating a well in the middle.

7

Place a teaspoon of the sweetened cream cheese and a tablespoon of the pineapple jam into each mold.

8

Refrigerate for 1 hour. Gently lift out the pineapple tarts by pulling the wax paper up. Place on a plate and serve.

You don't need an oven to make these tasty tarts!

Balinese
Banana Pancakes

The most delicious banana pancakes can be found in **Bali**, one of the islands of Indonesia. Made with soft, sweet bananas this is a wonderful taste sensation.

Ingredients

3 ripe bananas
1 cup (5 oz/150 g) flour
1 tablespoon superfine sugar
1/2 teaspoon salt
1 teaspoon baking powder
1 egg
2 tablespoons melted butter
   or vegetable oil
1/2 teaspoon vanilla extract
3/4 cup (200 ml) coconut milk
   or milk
Oil for greasing the skillet
Honey or maple syrup

Utensils

4 x

Anneke is wearing a colorful *sarong* (a kind of wraparound skirt) and a blouse called a *kebaya*.

Balinese women carry tall offerings of cakes and fruits to the village temple on festival days. Almost every day there is a temple festival somewhere in Bali!

30 min

1

Peel 2 of the bananas and place them on a plate. Using a fork, mash the bananas.

2

Put the flour, sugar, salt and baking powder into a bowl. Stir with a spoon to mix well.

Other Fruits

In place of bananas you can also try other fruits like mangoes, blueberries or apple slices.

4 Pieces

3

Add the mashed bananas, egg, melted butter or oil and vanilla extract to the flour mixture.

4

Add the coconut milk or milk and stir with a wooden spoon until there are no lumps.

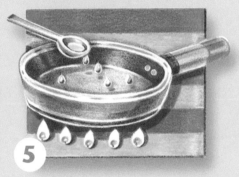

5

Place a skillet on the stove and turn the heat to medium. Let it heat up for 1 minute then add a few drops of oil to grease the skillet.

You get the nicest pancakes when you use low or medium heat

6

Scoop 1 ladle of the batter into the skillet. Use the back of the ladle or gently swirl the pan to spread the pancake batter into a round shape.

7

Make sure the skillet is not too hot. Turn the heat down a bit if necessary. Let the pancake cook on one side for about 1 minute and then, using a spatula, turn it over to cook on the other side.

8

Place the pancake on a serving plate. Peel and slice the other banana and place the slices on top of the pancakes. Drizzle with maple syrup or honey.

Learning About Asian Ingredients

Blanched almonds are almonds that have been quickly boiled to remove the skins. You can buy them in supermarkets, and they are usually sold in cans or plastic bags. Alternatively, to make them yourself boil a few cups of water and pour it over raw almonds in a bowl. Soak for 5 minutes, and when cool, rub the skins off.

Bok choy and **choy sum** are two common types of Asian leafy green vegetables. Bok choy leaves are dark green and spoon shaped. Choy sum has thinner, lighter green leaves. Bok choy and choy sum are both available in most large supermarkets. Use Chinese cabbage or spinach as a substitute.

Cardamom is a spice with a warm lemony flavor. Ground cardamom powder is sold bottled in most supermarkets. Use ground cinnamon as a substitute.

Coriander leaves, also known as cilantro or Chinese parsley, are a leafy green herb with a mild taste, used mainly as a garnish. Look for them in the fresh produce section of your supermarket. Fresh coriander leaves should keep for 5 to 6 days if you wash and dry the leaves and keep them in the fridge in a plastic bag.

Dashi is a Japanese soup stock made from edible seaweed and flakes of dried bonito tunafish and water. Instant dashi, dashi powder or dashi granules, which can simply be mixed with hot water to make dashi stock, is sold in small bottles or cans in Asian food stores. Use chicken or vegetable soup stock or bouillon cubes as a substitute.

Lemongrass is a long, lemon-scented stalk that is used to season and enhance the flavor of many dishes. Use only the lower part of the stalk. Remove the dried outer layers, then slice or smash the tender inner part for use. Lemongrass is available fresh, frozen or dried, but fresh lemongrass is preferred as it has a stronger aroma and flavor.

Nori sheets are thin sheets of dried seaweed, dark green in color, with the natural taste of the sea. The sheets look like dark green paper and are sold in plastic packets. There are different types—look for roasted or dried seaweed on the package—as both can be used for making sushi rolls. Nori sheets are found in Asian markets or the Asian section of large grocery stores.

Dried rice paper wrappers are paperlike sheets, white in color, made from rice flour, water and salt. They are brittle, ultrathin and semitransparent. To use the dried wrappers you must first soften them in warm water. Look for rice paper wrappers in supermarkets and Asian stores. They are sold in plastic packets of 10 or 20.

Sesame oil, pressed from sesame seeds, comes in two varieties: light sesame oil, which has a mild nutty flavor, and dark sesame oil, which is darker in color and has a stronger flavor. Dark sesame oil, also known as Chinese sesame oil, is made from toasted sesame seeds. Sesame oil is sold bottled in most large supermarkets or Asian stores.

Shiitake mushrooms are sold fresh or dried and are golden brown to dark brown in color. Dried shiitake mushrooms must be first soaked in hot water for about 10 minutes to soften them. Discard the stems and use only the caps. Fresh shiitake mushrooms are available in most supermarkets, and dried mushrooms are found in Asian specialty stores.

Soft or silken tofu (beancurd) is slippery and tends to crumble easily. It is a bit like soft cheese in texture. Soft tofu is sold in water-filled plastic tubs or tubes in the refrigerated section of supermarkets or Asian specialty stores. Store it refrigerated and immersed in water.

Tahini is a sesame paste made from ground roasted sesame seeds. It is available fresh, in cans or jars. Tahini can be found in health food stores, supermarkets and specialty food stores.

Wasabi, also known as Japanese horseradish, is bright green in color and has a sharp taste like hot mustard. It is used in dressings, dips and sauces. In Japan, fresh wasabi root is normally grated with special tiny graters and served with sushi and noodle dishes. Wasabi paste is sold in plastic squeeze tubes, while wasabi powder is sold in small cans in supermarkets or specialty stores. Add water to the powder to make wasabi paste, following the directions on the can. Hot mustard can be used instead of wasabi.

Wonton wrappers are small, thin sheets of dough, tan in color, and made from flour, eggs and water. Wonton wrappers are sold fresh or frozen in plastic packets in supermarkets.

Measurement Conversions

All our recipes are thoroughly tested in the Periplus test kitchen. Standard metric measuring cups and spoons are used throughout, and all cup and spoon measurements are level. We have used medium-sized (60 g, grade 3) eggs in all recipes.

International Measures

1 cup	= 8 fl oz (250 ml)
1 teaspoon	= 5 ml
1 UK/US tablespoon	= 15 ml (3 teaspoons)
1 Australian tablespoon	= 20 ml (4 teaspoons)

Weights	Volumes	Lengths
28 g = 1 oz	30 ml = 1 fl oz	3 mm = $\frac{1}{8}$ inch
225 g = 8 oz	125 ml = 4 fl oz	6 mm = $\frac{1}{4}$ inch
450 g = 16 oz	250 ml = 8 fl oz	1 cm = $\frac{1}{2}$ inch
		2.5 cm = 1 inch

We have used international 15 ml tablespoon measures. If you are using an Australian 20 ml tablespoon, the difference will not be noticeable for most recipes. However, for recipes using flour, cornstarch and baking powder, subtract one teaspoon for each tablespoon specified.

Oven Temperature Guide

As cooking times often vary slightly depending on the type of oven used, it is advisable to check the manufacturer's instructions to ensure proper temperature control. When using convection ovens, the top of the food may cook too quickly. As a general rule, set the oven temperature 59°F (15°C) to 68°F (20°C) lower than the temperature indicated in the recipe, or refer to your oven manual.

	°F	°C
Cool	200	100
Slow	300	150
Warm	325	170
Moderate	350	180
Moderately hot	375	190
Moderately hot	400	200
Hot	425	220
Very hot	450	230